A DAILY SEED WILL BRING A DAILY HARVEST

Dr. Jason Martin Sr.

Jason Martin Ministries
13917 Smokey Point Blvd
Marysville, Wa 98332
www.drjasonmartin.org
dr.Jasonmartin@outlook.com

FOREWORD

A Daily Seed Will Bring a Daily Harvest

In a world where many search for shortcuts to success, **A Daily Seed Will Bring a Daily Harvest** by my spiritual son, Dr Jason Martin, Sr., stands as both a roadmap and a testimony. This is not merely a book of principles—it is the lived experience of a man who practices what he teaches. Dr Martin is a living example of the power of daily sowing. His life reflects the very truths laid out in these pages: discipline, faith, consistency, and the unshakable belief that God always honors the seeds we sow.

Across these chapters, Dr Martin reveals the spiritual and practical insights that brilliantly transformed his own life. He begins with "The Revelation of Daily Sowing," a foundational truth that sets the tone for the journey ahead. From there, he walks the reader through timeless laws— like "The Law That Never Fails" and the truth that "What You Sow Into, You Grow Into." These are not theories; they are spiritual laws that have shaped destinies for generations.

His transparency shines through in chapters like *"How I Got Free by Matching My Offering With My Tithe"* and *"Dressed Up Poverty,"* where he confronts the illusions that hold many back. Dr Martin does not shy away from bold, faith-filled declarations such as "Wealth & Riches Shall Be in Your House" and "From Not Enough to More Than

Enough," reminding us that God's desire is not scarcity but abundance.

Every chapter builds upon the next, demonstrating how God works through obedience, sacrifice, and trust. He reminds us in "If God Doesn't Work, Nothing Works" that our efforts are meaningless without divine partnership. He challenges believers in "Don't Keep Sowing on the Same Level," urging them to cultivate spiritual and financial maturity. And he closes in strength with truths such as "God Multiplies the Seed You Sow," the central message of "A Daily Seed Brings a Daily Harvest," and the heart-exposing question, "How Much Money Is in Your Heart for God?"

Ultimately, this book is for the person who longs to live out Deuteronomy 8:18—to remember the Lord their God, who gives power to get wealth, not for self-glory, but to establish His covenant on the earth. Dr Martin's teachings provide a clear, practical, and biblical pathway for anyone ready to take that step.

If you are seeking breakthrough, clarity, consistency, and a deeper walk with God in financial stewardship, this book will water the seeds of your faith. I challenge you to read it with expectation...apply it with diligence... and watch God honor your seed—daily!

— Archbishop H. Michael Chitwood, ThD, DDiv.
Founder and President
International Congress of Churches & Ministers

DEDICATION

To my wife Ramona — my covenant partner,
my encourager, my best friend.

Your faith, love, and courage have been a daily
seed in my life.

ACKNOWLEDGMENTS

I want to thank my Kingdom Church International family for believing, sowing, and walking this journey with me. To my spiritual father, Dr. H. Michael Chitwood—thank you for imparting wisdom and accountability that sharpened my stewardship. I honor my mentors from the U.S. Navy and the Seattle FBI Citizens Academy for instilling discipline, courage, and excellence.

To my medical team and transplant community—your hands were guided by God when, in 2021, I received a new heart in three days after being told it could take years. I give glory to God for the miracle and thank every person He used.

Finally, to every reader who has ever wrestled with not-enough: this book is my seed into your future. May it multiply a hundredfold.

TABLE OF CONTENTS

INTRODUCTION

Hi, I'm Jason Martin Sr., and before I introduce myself, let me ask you a question:

Are you ready to go from nowhere financially to somewhere? From a financial nobody to a financial somebody? From poverty to prosperity?

Great. Then you're holding a book that will reorder your financial world. I spent years on welfare, struggling to meet basic needs while pastoring and raising a family. But God opened my eyes to a simple, unstoppable principle: a daily seed will bring a daily harvest (Ecclesiastes 11:6; Genesis 8:22).

As I obeyed—sowing consistently, listening for instruction, and stewarding the harvest—my life was transformed. God gave me Revelation from Deuteronomy 8:18: "It is He that giveth thee power to get wealth." That Power flows through the seed you sow and the wisdom you obey.

This is not a theory book. It's a field guide drenched in testimony, Scripture, and repeatable steps.

Read, apply, and watch God's faithfulness meet your diligence.

CHAPTER 1
THE REVELATION OF DAILY SOWING

Scripture Foundation

Ecclesiastes 11:6 (KJV):

"In the morning sow thy seed, and in the evening withhold not thine hand."

Genesis 8:22 (KJV):

"While the earth remaineth, seedtime and harvest... shall not cease."

Hook

Have you ever wanted constant blessing but only sowed occasionally? You tithed faithfully, gave in special offerings, and maybe even planted a big seed once in a while—but deep down, you knew there had to be more.

God's harvest law isn't seasonal—it's daily. The Kingdom of God operates on rhythm, not randomness. If you want daily harvests, you must practice daily sowing. Not random bursts—daily rhythms.

That's the law of daily sowing: making generosity a lifestyle instead of an event.

My Story

Before I discovered the power of daily sowing, my giving was inconsistent. I gave when I felt inspired or when there was a special service. I gave when I could, and withheld when things were tight. I called it "being wise," but really, it was fear disguised as logic.

The result? My harvests were unpredictable. Some months overflowed with favor, and others felt dry and empty. I prayed for financial consistency, but my sowing wasn't consistent. I was asking God to honor a principle I wasn't practicing daily.

Then one morning, while in prayer, I heard the Holy Spirit say, "A daily seed will bring a daily harvest."

At first, I didn't understand. Daily? Every day? How would that even work? I thought giving was for Sundays and special offerings, not Mondays through Saturdays.

But the Lord reminded me of Ecclesiastes 11:6—"In the morning sow thy seed, and in the evening withhold not thine hand." The verse didn't say *sow when it's convenient*; it said *in the morning and evening*. That's a daily rhythm.

So I made a decision. I chose an amount I could release every day—not a large sum, but a consistent one—and I started sowing intentionally. I gave into my church, and my spiritual father, when the Spirit prompted me. I attached every seed to a purpose: becoming debt free, family legacy, ministry expansion and building my own financial portfolio

At first, it felt simple. Then it became sacred. Each seed became a daily act of worship.

And soon, I started seeing daily testimonies—unexpected favor, divine ideas, open doors, and supernatural provision. The fog of "someday" lifted. The act of sowing daily didn't just change my finances—it changed my faith. I stopped waiting for harvests and started walking in them.

That's the power of daily sowing. It trains your heart to live in faith every single day.

Scripture & Teaching

Sowing is a Law, Not a Lottery – "Be not deceived; God is not mocked: for whatsoever a man soweth, that shall he also reap" (Galatians 6:7 KJV).

Sowing isn't a gamble—it's a guarantee. The principle of seedtime and harvest is as fixed as gravity. It's not about luck or chance; it's about law. When you treat giving as a law, you stop waiting for miracles to "happen" and start expecting them to *manifest*.

Consistency consistently outperforms intensity. Anyone can give once in excitement, but true faith is measured by what you do repeatedly. Daily sowing is proof that you trust the system God designed more than the emotions you feel.

Your Schedule Is Your Theology in Motion – "In due season we shall reap, if we faint not" (Galatians 6:9 KJV).

Your calendar reveals what you believe. If sowing is a divine law, it deserves a space in your daily schedule.

Don't relegate it to impulse or inspiration—schedule it like prayer, work, or family.

When you add sowing to your daily routine, it transforms from duty to delight. You start looking forward to it because every seed becomes a faith statement: *"God, I trust You again today."*

Assign Your Seed a Mission – "Write the vision and make it plain..." (Habakkuk 2:2 KJV).

Every seed has potential, but only a directed seed has purpose. Don't just give randomly—give intentionally. Assign your seed a mission.

Write it down:
"This seed is for my prosperous financial future."
"This seed is for debt cancellation."
"This seed is for ministry expansion."
"This seed is for healing in my body."

When you give your seed a name, it gives your faith an aim. God doesn't just bless giving—He blesses purpose-driven giving.

Obedience Outlasts Emotion

Let's be honest—there will be days when you don't *feel* like sowing. Days when the bills look bigger than your faith. Days when your emotions shout louder than your spirit. But daily sowing isn't about feelings—it's about faithfulness.

Every time you sow in faith, you say to God, "I trust Your law more than my lack."

Some days your seed may be small, others larger—but obedience always carries weight in Heaven. Remember: a seed may leave your hand, but it never leaves your life. It travels into your future, multiplies under divine supervision, and comes back in the form of harvest.

Summary

- Daily sowing creates daily harvests.
- Sowing is a law, not a lottery—consistency dominates intensity.
- Your schedule reveals your faith.
- Assign your seed a mission and expect multiplication.
- Obedience will take you where emotion cannot.
- A seed may leave your hand, but it never leaves your life.

Reflection Questions

1. Have I been sowing consistently, or only when it feels convenient?
2. Where in my day can I schedule a non-negotiable sowing moment?
3. What outcomes do I want my seed to target over the next 90 days?
4. How can I make sowing a consistent expression of trust, not a moment of impulse?

Faith Action

Create a 30-day sowing plan. Write it out clearly:

Time – Will I sow in the morning, at lunch, or before bed?

Amount – What can I commit to daily without fear, but with faith?

Intention – What do I believe God will bring forth from this seed?

Treat this plan like a covenant, not a challenge. Track what happens. Journal the results. Watch how small, daily obedience produces supernatural patterns of increase. Your future will be filled with the fruit of the faith you practice every day.

Closing Prayer

Father, engrave daily sowing into my heart and habits. Teach my hands to sow and my spirit to expect. Let every seed I release produce a daily harvest of provision, peace, and purpose.

I refuse to give by impulse—I choose to sow by instruction. Let every act of obedience position me for overflow. I declare that my schedule reflects my faith, and my seed guarantees my future. Thank You for multiplying what I release into Kingdom soil.

In Jesus' name, Amen.

Next Chapter Teaser

You've learned the law of daily sowing—the rhythm that sustains harvests. In the next chapter, we'll uncover *the law that never fails* and how to cooperate with it until abundance becomes your lifestyle.

CHAPTER 2

THE LAW THAT NEVER FAILS

Scripture Foundation

Numbers 23:19 (KJV):

"God is not a man, that he should lie."

Galatians 6:7 (KJV):

"Be not deceived; God is not mocked: for whatsoever a man soweth, that shall he also reap."

Hook

When God binds a promise to a principle, results become inevitable for the obedient. The law of sowing and reaping is one of those divine guarantees. It does not bend to emotion or circumstance—it operates on obedience and time. When you understand that this law never fails, your faith stops wavering and your confidence starts growing.

My Story

There was a time when I doubted if my giving really made a difference. I would sow, wait, and wonder. Some seeds seemed to produce overnight, while others took months or even years to show fruit.

In my leanest season, I sowed when it felt foolish—when bills were high and emotions low. Yet even in those moments, something in me knew: if God established this law, it could not fail.

The outcomes were slow—then sudden. Just when I thought nothing was moving, everything shifted. Opportunities opened, debts cleared, favor multiplied.

God wasn't late; He was aligning my faith, my habits, and my field. I realized that my job was not to make the law work—it already worked. My responsibility was to cooperate with it consistently.

Scripture & Teaching

The law of sowing and reaping isn't human—it's divine. It existed before nations, economies, or systems. Genesis 8:22 declared it plainly: "While the earth remaineth, seedtime and harvest shall not cease."

That means the law works in every generation, in every location, and under every condition.

Numbers 23:19 (KJV) says, "God is not a man, that He should lie." That single verse anchors our confidence. If He spoke a law, it is unbreakable. The same God who made gravity made generosity.

Just as you never doubt whether gravity will hold you to the ground, you should never doubt that sowing will bring reaping.

Galatians 6:7 reminds us: "God is not mocked." In other words, God will never allow His system to be proven wrong.

When you sow in faith, He ensures that seed produces after its kind.

Your consistency is the demonstration of your confidence in His truth.

Teaching & Application

The Law Works Even When Feelings Don't – Your emotions do not dictate your harvest. Feelings fluctuate, but faith must remain steady.

You may feel unseen, unheard, or unappreciated—but the soil never forgets a seed. God honors obedience, not mood swings.

Obedience outruns emotion, and when you stay faithful, your consistency becomes prophetic evidence that you believe the law still works.

Delay is NOT Denial – Seeds take time to germinate. Just because you don't see growth doesn't mean nothing is happening.

Farmers don't dig up their seeds every day to check progress—they trust the process. Likewise, your seed is working beneath the surface even when circumstances seem unchanged.

Ecclesiastes 3:1 reminds us, "To everything there is a season." When your season comes, harvest will appear suddenly, though it has been growing silently all along.

Guard Your Confession – Proverbs 18:21 declares that "death and life are in the power of the tongue."

Your words are the climate of your harvest. When you speak doubt, you dry out your soil. When you speak faith, you water it.

Confession isn't empty repetition—it's divine alignment. Your mouth is a seed sower, too. What you continually declare shapes the field your life will reap.

✅ Summary

- God cannot lie. His law of sowing and reaping cannot fail.
- When you obey consistently, results become inevitable.
- Emotions may shift, but obedience holds steady.
- Delay is not denial—your seed is working beneath the soil.
- Guard your confession; your words determine your harvest atmosphere.
- The law that never fails is already at work for those who refuse to quit.

✏️ Reflection Questions

1. Where have I allowed delay to change my confession?
2. Which promises anchor my sowing during quiet seasons?
3. What daily habits prove that I trust God's law even when results seem slow?
4. How can I strengthen my confession so that my words align with my faith?

5. What area of my life is ready for a harvest that obedience will unlock?

Faith Action

Write a harvest confession based on God's promises and speak it morning and evening for 30 days.

Use Scriptures like Numbers 23:19, Galatians 6:7, and Genesis 8:22 to declare that the law of sowing and reaping never fails.

Speak faith, not frustration. Expect manifestation, not explanation.

Record any changes, testimonies, or breakthroughs you experience during this period. Your words will prepare your world for increase.

🙏 Closing Prayer

God of truth, stabilize my heart in Your unbreakable law. Forgive me for every moment of doubt and impatience.

Teach me to wait with expectation, to speak with faith, and to sow with confidence. I declare that Your Word is final, Your law is working, and my harvest is sure.

You are not a man that You should lie, and You are not mocked. My seed will produce, my words will agree, and my harvest will manifest.

In Jesus' name, Amen.

◉ Next Chapter Teaser

You've learned the law that never fails—God's system of truth and timing.

In the next chapter, we'll explore how what you sow into, you grow into—and how your partnerships, environments, and giving connections shape your future harvest.

CHAPTER 3
WHAT YOU SOW INTO, YOU GROW INTO

Scripture Foundation

2 Corinthians 9:6–8 (KJV):

"But this I say, He which soweth sparingly shall reap also sparingly; and he which soweth bountifully shall reap also bountifully.

Every man according as he purposeth in his heart, so let him give; not grudgingly, or of necessity: for God loveth a cheerful giver.

And God is able to make all grace abound toward you; that ye, always having all sufficiency in all things, may abound to every good work."

Proverbs 11:24–25 (KJV):

"There is that scattereth, and yet increaseth; and there is that withholdeth more than is meet, but it tendeth to poverty.

The liberal soul shall be made fat: and he that watereth shall be watered also himself."

Hook

Your seed shapes you before it funds you.

Giving isn't only about what leaves your hand—it's about what grows in your heart.

Every time you sow, you're not just releasing money—you're reinforcing identity.

What you sow into determines what grows within you.

My Story

When I first started sowing daily, my giving was sincere—but scattered. I sowed wherever I felt inspired. Sometimes into ministries, sometimes into people, sometimes into my spiritual leaders. And while God honored every seed, I began to notice something: my harvests were as scattered as my sowing.

Then one morning, in prayer, the Holy Spirit gave me a simple but life-changing revelation: "What you sow into, you grow into."

That phrase shifted everything. I realized that seed is not only financial - It's what God uses to shape our future. Every seed carries the DNA of what it's planted into. If I wanted to grow as a pastor, I needed to sow into pastors. If I wanted to grow as a builder and entrepreneur, I needed to sow into those who carried that grace.

So I began to focus my giving intentionally. I identified the areas of my life I wanted to see expand—spiritual leadership, business vision, and family impact. I started sowing consistently into proven pastors, and spiritual leaders that were where I wanted to be in life.

Over time, something remarkable happened. My perspective changed. My wisdom multiplied. My capacity stretched. The very anointings I sowed into began to manifest in my own life.

As I focused my seed on pastors, entrepreneurs, and families, I grew into a shepherd-builder—someone with vision for both ministry and enterprise. That's when I learned: your seed doesn't just leave your life—it shapes your future self.

Scripture & Teaching

Targeted Seed Creates Targeted Growth – 2 Corinthians 9:6–8 teaches that giving is proportional: "He which soweth bountifully shall reap also bountifully." But bountiful isn't just about *amount*—it's about *alignment*. When you direct your seed toward specific graces, you reap in that same grace.

Sow into wisdom, and you grow in understanding. Sow into faith, and you expand in boldness. Sow into excellence, and you rise in influence.

If You Want a Mentor's Grace, Sow Into That Grace – Philippians 4:17–19 shows us that when the church gave to Paul, they didn't just meet his needs—they partook in his anointing. "Not that I desire a gift, but I desire fruit that may abound to your account."

When you sow into a leader or ministry, you participate in their fruit. The grace on their life begins to grow in yours.

Stop Scattering Everywhere; Choose Strategic Fields – Proverbs 11:24–25 reminds us that those who give strategically "increase." Growth comes from focus, not frenzy. Too many believers scatter seed without purpose, then wonder why harvest feels random.

Strategic sowing creates structured growth. When you commit to specific, fertile fields, your faith stops being emotional and starts being intentional.

Teaching & Application

- **Targeted Seed Creates Targeted Growth.** Stop giving aimlessly—attach your seed to your assignment.
- **If You Want a Mentor's Grace, Sow Into That Grace.** Honor attracts impartation. What you respect, you reflect.
- **Stop Scattering Everywhere; Choose Strategic Fields.** Three focused fields outperform thirty random ones. Be deliberate.
- **Your Seed Determines Your Shape.** Every seed carries the nature of the soil it's planted in—choose wisely.
- **Partnership Produces Parallels.** The people you sow into influence what manifests in you.

Summary

Your seed determines your growth pattern.

Sowing isn't just financial—it's life changing.

When you sow into wisdom, you grow wise. When you sow into faith, you become bold. When you sow into excellence, you reflect excellence.

You grow in the direction of your generosity.

Focused sowing builds focused growth, and partnership multiplies grace.

What you sow into, you grow into.

Reflection Questions

- Who carries the grace I need to grow into?
- Which fields will I commit to for a full year?
- What character must grow in me to steward the harvest I seek?
- Am I sowing from emotion or intention?
- How does my current giving reveal what I'm growing toward?

Faith Action

Choose which Ministries, leaders that match your calling and assignment. I encourage you to start with a leader or ministry that believes in Seedtime and Harvest.

Set recurring gifts (weekly or monthly) to those fields for one full year.

Record the lessons, opportunities, and transformations that occur as a result.

Intentional sowing builds intentional growth. Over time, you'll discover that you don't just give to needs—you sow into your own becoming.

⛪ Closing Prayer

Father, align my seed with my calling so I grow into Your design. Teach me to sow strategically, faithfully, and joyfully.

Let every seed I plant produce the character, capacity, and calling You've ordained for me.

Help me to identify the right fields, connect with the right voices, and grow into the person You created me to be.

In Jesus' name, Amen.

➲ Next Chapter Teaser

You've learned how to grow through what you sow—how targeted seed creates targeted increase. In the next chapter, I'll take you to the turning point of my journey—the day I began *matching my offering with my tithe*, and how that single act unlocked supernatural acceleration.

CHAPTER 4

HOW I GOT FREE BY MATCHING MY OFFERING WITH MY TITHE

Scripture Foundation

Malachi 3:10–12 (KJV):

"Bring ye all the tithes into the storehouse, that there may be meat in mine house, and prove me now herewith, saith the Lord of hosts, if I will not open you the windows of heaven, and pour you out a blessing, that there shall not be room enough to receive it. And I will rebuke the devourer for your sakes, and he shall not destroy the fruits of your ground; neither shall your vine cast her fruit before the time in the field, saith the Lord of hosts. And all nations shall call you blessed: for ye shall be a delightsome land, saith the Lord of hosts."

Luke 6:38 (KJV):

"Give, and it shall be given unto you; good measure, pressed down, and shaken together, and running over, shall men give into your bosom. For with the same measure that ye mete withal it shall be measured to you again."

Hook

There's a moment when giving moves from obligation to revelation. For me, that moment came the day I matched my offering with my tithe. Until then, I gave faithfully, but not fearlessly. The day I decided that my offering would equal—or exceed—my tithe, financial momentum changed. Heaven didn't just open; it accelerated.

My Story

For years, I was faithful in tithing but frustrated in living. I preached prosperity while privately juggling bills. As a pastor, I wanted my congregation to see faithfulness in me—but I was living from welfare to welfare, paycheck to paycheck.

One afternoon, I stood in the grocery store wearing my best suit, but inwardly feeling the weight of financial lack. At the checkout counter, I reached for food stamps. That moment broke something in me. I whispered, "God, this cannot be the image of Your Kingdom. I'm thankful I can feed my family, but there has to be more."

Not long after that prayer, the Spirit of God spoke clearly to my heart: "Start matching your offering with your tithe."

It didn't make sense. How could I give more when I already felt like I had so little? But the instruction was clear—and I obeyed.

The first time I matched my offering with my tithe, something shifted. It wasn't just money leaving my hand; it was bondage leaving my life. My giving went from routine to revelatory. I discovered that the tithe acknowledged God's ownership—but the offering proved my trust in His provision.

That decision became the pivot that broke financial stagnation. My bills didn't vanish overnight, but the flow began. Unexpected blessings showed up. Ideas started producing. Needs were met before they became emergencies. My faith, not just my finances, began to multiply.

Looking back, I realize the key wasn't the amount—it was the obedience. God wasn't trying to take from me; He was teaching me to live beyond the limits of reason and fear. The tithe connected me to covenant, but the offering connected me to overflow.

Scripture & Teaching

The Tithe Keeps Covenant Alignment – Malachi 3:10–12 reveals that the tithe opens the windows of heaven and rebukes the devourer. The tithe doesn't make you rich—it makes you protected. It positions your life under the covering of divine partnership. When you return the tenth, you acknowledge that God owns it all.

The Offering Unlocks Multiplication – Luke 6:38 shows us the next level: the law of increase. The offering isn't about paying dues; it's about planting seed. The measure you give determines the measure you live on. The tithe maintains; the offering multiplies.

Matching Breaks Mental Ceilings – When you match your offering with your tithe, you confront fear directly.

You tell scarcity that it no longer governs your generosity. Matching offerings trains your faith to expect more—and it shifts your mindset from survival to expansion.

Start Where You're at, Grow Past It by Faith – God never measures your seed by size, but by sacrifice. Matching your offering to your tithe is a starting point, not a ceiling. Over time, as your faith grows, your generosity will outgrow your income. That's how abundance becomes a rhythm, not an event.

Teaching & Application

- **Tithe = Covenant Acknowledgment (Protection).** It declares, "God, I trust You as my Source."
- **Offerings = Vision Expansion (Provision).** They say, "God, I'm ready for increase."
- **Matching Breaks Fear.** It renews your mind to think like a giver, not a survivor.
- **Get Started.** Match your tithe. Then, by faith, grow beyond it. Don't limit your generosity to comfort.
- **Expect Evidence.** Matching creates measurable testimonies. You'll see divine timing, provision, and creative ideas begin to flow.

Summary

- Tithing acknowledges covenant; offerings activate overflow.
- When you match your offering with your tithe, you break the ceiling of fear and move from maintenance to multiplication.

- God's system is simple: the tithe protects, the offering produces.
- Matching generosity proves maturity—it's the bridge between obedience and abundance.
- The same God who opened the windows of heaven in Malachi 3 is still pouring out blessings today for those who dare to give boldly.

Reflection Questions

1. What has kept me from pairing my offerings with my tithe?
2. Where has fear capped my giving level?
3. What faith target could my offerings accelerate?
4. Am I giving from comfort or conviction?
5. How would my finances change if obedience became my default?

Faith Action

For the next eight weeks, match (or exceed) your offerings to your tithe and journal the results.

Track your giving, your thoughts, and your testimonies. Write down every unexpected blessing, breakthrough, or opportunity that arises.

This exercise isn't about formulas—it's about faith formation. As you stay consistent, you'll notice not only external provision but internal transformation. Your generosity will become a declaration: *"God can trust me with increase."*

🙏 Closing Prayer

Lord, thank You for teaching me the power of matching my tithe with my offering. You are not trying to take from me—you are preparing to flow through me.

I choose obedience over fear and consistency over convenience. Teach me to sow boldly, trust deeply, and give joyfully.

Let every offering I release be a key that unlocks new levels of faith, favor, and financial freedom.

In Jesus' name, Amen.

🔵 Next Chapter Teaser

You've learned the freedom that comes from matching your offering with your tithe. In the next chapter, we'll explore how to pursue *excellence without pretense*—no more gold-plated luxury, but true Kingdom excellence that honors God and transforms lives.

CHAPTER 5

DRESSED UP POVERTY

Hook

Have you ever looked the part of prosperity while secretly living in lack? You smiled, you dressed well, you carried yourself with confidence — but inside you were weighed down by financial struggle.

That's what I call dressed-up poverty — a polished image on the outside, hidden shame on the inside, and pockets that don't reflect how you look.

My Story

I know precisely what dressed-up poverty looks like because it was on me as a pastor. I will never forget standing in the grocery store, dressed in my suit, looking prosperous — but I was broke. I walked the aisles like everything was fine, but when I got to the checkout counter, I had to pay for my groceries with food stamps.

In that moment, I felt ashamed and embarrassed. I whispered, "God, I'm thankful I can feed my family, but this is not a good image of Your Kingdom. Something has to change. Please show me what I need to do."

Not long after that prayer, I heard the Spirit of God say:

"Start matching your offering with your tithe." That one instruction marked a turning point in my financial journey.

Scripture & Teaching

Paul wrote in Romans 12:2 (NKJV):

"Do not be conformed to this world, but be transformed by the renewing of your mind."

Conforming means copying the world's system — where appearances matter more than truth. Transformation happens when we live by Kingdom principles.

Here are three practical keys to breaking free from dressed up poverty:

1. Understand the Role of the Tithe – The tithe belongs to God (Leviticus 27:30 NKJV). It doesn't make you rich — it keeps you in covenant alignment. The tithe opens the windows of heaven (Malachi 3:10 NKJV).
2. Unlock Increase with the Offering – The offering is where multiplication begins. Jesus said, "Give, and it will be given to you: good measure, pressed down, shaken together, and running over" (Luke 6:38 NKJV). Paul added, "He who sows sparingly will also reap sparingly, and he who sows bountifully will also reap bountifully" (2 Corinthians 9:6 NKJV).
3. Refuse to Fake Prosperity – True blessing adds no sorrow with it (Proverbs 10:22 NKJV). Dressed up poverty might fool people, but it doesn't glorify God. Real prosperity is visible, tangible, and undeniable — it's peace, provision, and overflow.

◉ Summary

- Dressed up poverty is projecting prosperity while living in lack — an image that misrepresents God's Kingdom.
- My turning point came in a grocery store — suited up, paying with food stamps — followed by a prayer that led to the instruction: "Match your offering with your tithe."
- Romans 12:2 (NKJV) calls us from conformity (image management) to transformation (Kingdom manifestation).
- The tithe keeps covenant alignment and opens the windows (Leviticus 27:30 NKJV; Malachi 3:10 NKJV); the offering determines the measure of the harvest (Luke 6:38 NKJV; 2 Corinthians 9:6 NKJV).
- True prosperity is peace, provision, and overflow without sorrow (Proverbs 10:22 NKJV) — something you can't fake but must cultivate through obedience, stewardship, and generosity.

✎ Reflection Questions

1. Have I ever found myself projecting prosperity while secretly struggling?
2. What emotions rise up in me when I compare my financial image versus my financial reality?
3. Am I honoring God with both my tithe and my offering? If not, what step can I take today to begin?
4. How would my life change if I walked in true prosperity that adds no sorrow?

🙏 Closing Prayer

Father, in Jesus' Name, I renounce the trap of dressed up poverty. Forgive me for every time I settled for an image of prosperity without the reality of it. Lord, I choose today to honor You with my tithe and my offering. Teach me to sow with faith and obedience, and let my life reflect Your Kingdom prosperity.

Just as you gave Jason a new house and a new heart, I believe You will do the same for me. I declare that shame, lack, and hidden struggle will no longer define me. I am blessed to be a blessing.

Amen.

➡ Next Chapter Teaser

You've just learned how to break free from the image of prosperity without the reality of it. But God doesn't just want to remove poverty — He wants to establish wealth and riches in your house. In the next chapter, we will explore what true Kingdom wealth looks like and how to walk in it confidently.

CHAPTER 6

WEALTH AND RICHES SHALL BE IN YOUR HOUSE

Scripture Foundation

"Wealth and riches will be in his house, and his righteousness endures forever."
— Psalm 112:3 (NKJV)

Hook

This scripture turned my life around. Too many Christians talk about being "blessed," but their lives don't show it. God never called us to just quote prosperity — He called us to demonstrate prosperity.

God's Plan: Overflow in Your House

Notice Psalm 112:3 (NKJV) doesn't say wealth and riches will be in the government, in the bank, or in somebody else's house. It says wealth and riches will be in your house.

That means your home is meant to be a place of abundance, provision, and overflow. And not just your physical house — your body is God's house too. He intends for both your finances and your health to overflow with Kingdom blessing.

My Testimony: From Welfare to Wealth

For years, my house was a house of struggle. I lived on welfare for a decade. Bills piled up, and I felt the constant pressure of not having enough.

But everything changed when I committed to daily sowing. I didn't just tithe faithfully; I began to sow consistent daily seeds in the morning and at night, just like Ecclesiastes 11:6 (NKJV) says.

As I matched my offerings with my tithe, God shifted my financial destiny. I went from renting all my life to owning my first home — a 3,400 sq. ft. house on a golf course. That wasn't just a house; it was Psalm 112:3 (NKJV) coming alive in my life.

Wealth That Lasts vs. Wealth That Fades

- Worldly Wealth – temporary, unreliable, here today and gone tomorrow.
- Kingdom Wealth – lasting, multiplying, covenant-backed, and generational.

Proverbs 10:22 (NKJV) says:

"The blessing of the Lord makes one rich,
and He adds no sorrow with it."

Real prosperity doesn't just look good — it lasts, and it brings peace with it.

Practical Keys to Unlocking Wealth in Your House

1. Make Sowing a Daily Lifestyle – Daily financial seed guarantees continual harvest.
2. Sow Into Spiritual Leadership – Connect your seed to your pastor, the men and women of God.
3. Guard Against Poverty Thinking – Don't say, "I can't afford to sow." The truth is, you can't afford not to.
4. Expect Tangible Results – Believe for actual wealth, not just symbolic blessings.
5. Declare Psalm 112:3 (NKJV) Daily – Speak it until it manifests: "Wealth and riches are in my house."

My Testimony: A New Heart and No Debt

In 2021, I faced my greatest challenge. Doctors told me I needed a heart transplant. They said I'd be placed on the list, but it could take 3–5 years before a heart became available.

But just three days later, those same doctors walked into my room and said: "We found you a heart." Glory to God! What man said could take years, God provided in three days.

That surgery cost over $1.7 million — but as God is my witness, He supernaturally paid the entire bill. Today I carry no medical debt. I don't know which seed produced that harvest, but I know this: when I was dying, the seed gave me a new heart.

Psalm 112:3 (NKJV) doesn't just mean wealth and riches in your physical home. Your body is His house too. Just as He put a healthy, wealthy heart in my chest, He will put whatever you need in your house — healing, restoration, and life.

That's why I teach about the "Seal the Deal" seed. Whatever you are believing for — physically, mentally, emotionally, spiritually, or financially — you can seal it with a financial seed of faith. God is no respecter of persons. What He did for me, He's ready to do for you.

⊘ Takeaway Summary

- Psalm 112:3 (NKJV) is a covenant promise: wealth and riches in your house.
- This includes both your finances and your physical body.
- Daily sowing unlocks continual harvest.
- The same God who gave me a house and a heart can do it for you.

✎ Reflection Questions

1. Do I believe Psalm 112:3 (NKJV) applies to both my finances and my health?
2. What daily seed can I sow that declares wealth and riches are in my house?
3. Am I willing to sow a "Seal the Deal" seed for the breakthrough I need?

⚘ Prayer

Father, thank You for Your covenant promise in Psalm 112:3 (NKJV). I declare that wealth and riches are in my house — in my finances, in my family, and in my body. Just as You gave me a new house and a brand-new heart, I believe You are ready to do the same for me and for every person who sows in faith.

I sow today expecting supernatural harvests — physically, mentally, emotionally, spiritually, and financially.

In Jesus' name, Amen.

CHAPTER 7

FROM NOT ENOUGH TO MORE THAN ENOUGH

Hook

Have you ever been in a place where no matter how hard you worked, it was never enough? Bills stacked higher than your paycheck, needs bigger than your resources, and dreams constantly put on hold. That's the reality of not enough.

But here's the good news: God never intended for His children to live in "not enough." His plan has always been to bring you into more than enough.

My Story

I know what it feels like to live in not enough. There were seasons when I wondered how I would make it through the week, especially raising seven children on one family income. I remember walking into the grocery store dressed up in my suit, looking like I had it together — but when I got to the checkout counter, I had to pay for groceries with food stamps. Outwardly, I looked prosperous. Inwardly, I was in survival mode.

I whispered under my breath, "God, I'm thankful I can feed my family, but this is not a good image of Your Kingdom. Something has to change. Please show me what to do."

That cry became the beginning of my journey out of not enough. God began teaching me the law of sowing and reaping. At first, my seeds were small, and honestly, I was giving in desperation. But as I obeyed, God began moving me from not enough to just enough. And as I stayed consistent, He shifted me again — into more than enough.

Fast forward: Ramona and I, in addition to our daily seed, have now sown one-time seeds of $50,000 — twice. Once into a powerful and prosperous man of God, and once into our church. Then, in July 2021, after my heart transplant, the Lord gave me a vision and instructed me to sow $55,555 into my spiritual father. That seed wasn't random — it carried prophetic significance: 5 represents grace, and five fives represents grace multiplied.

When I started sowing in 2007, I never could have imagined giving $50,000 in a single seed. Back then, I could barely pay for groceries. But God cannot lie. His Word is true. And He took me step by step from not enough → just enough → more than enough → overflow.

Scripture & Teaching

1. God Supplies All Your Needs – "And my God shall supply all your need according to His riches in glory by Christ Jesus" (Philippians 4:19 NKJV). Your source isn't your paycheck — it's His riches in glory.
2. Jesus Multiplies What's in Your Hands – In John 6 (NKJV), a little boy's lunch fed over 5,000. When placed in Jesus' hands, "not enough" became more than enough.
3. God's Overflow Promise – "The Lord will open to

you His good treasure, the heavens, to give the rain to your land in its season and to bless all the work of your hand; you shall lend to many nations, but you shall not borrow" (Deuteronomy 28:12 NKJV). That's not survival — that's overflow.

4. Overflow is the Kingdom Standard – David declared in Psalm 23:5 (NKJV): "My cup runs over." Notice he didn't say, "My cup is full." Full means your needs are met. Overflow means you have more than enough to pour into others. God doesn't just want you sustained — He wants you spilling over with abundance so your life becomes a continual blessing to everyone around you.

5. Egypt → Wilderness → Promised Land – The story of Israel's journey paints a perfect picture of God's financial plan:

   - Egypt = Not Enough. They were slaves — working hard but never having enough to enjoy the fruit of their labor (Exodus 1:13–14 NKJV).
   - The Wilderness = Just Enough. God sent manna daily, but it was survival, not abundance (Exodus 16:35 NKJV). They always had what they needed for the day, but never more.
   - The Promised Land = More Than Enough. A land flowing with milk and honey, where vineyards already planted and houses already built awaited them (Deuteronomy 8:7–10 NKJV).

Egypt was not enough. The wilderness was just enough. But the Promised Land is more than enough. That's where God wants you to live today.

Practical Faith Actions

1. Stop Limiting God by What You See – Don't measure your future by your current bank account. Begin to see with eyes of faith that God's supply is greater than your need.
2. Put What You Have in God's Hands – Like the boy with the loaves and fish, take the little you have and release it to God through sowing. He cannot multiply what you refuse to place in His hands.
3. Live With a More Than Enough Mindset – Declare daily: "I serve the God of overflow. My cup runs over. I am moving from not enough to more than enough. I am blessed to be a blessing." Align your thoughts and words with God's abundance.

Summary

- The enemy's trap is not enough, but God's plan is more than enough.
- My journey proves this: from food stamps → daily seeds → breakthrough → sowing $50,000+ seeds.
- Philippians 4:19 (NKJV) reminds us that God's supply comes from His glory, not our paycheck.
- John 6 (NKJV) shows that when we give what we have to Jesus, He multiplies it.
- Deuteronomy 28:12 (NKJV) promises overflow blessings — lending and not borrowing.
- Psalm 23:5 (NKJV) reveals the Kingdom standard: not just full but running over.
- Israel's journey shows the progression: Egypt is not Enough, the Wilderness is Just Enough, and the Promised Land is more Than Enough.

- Faith actions of trust, sowing, and declaring overflow will shift you from lack to abundance.

✎ Reflection Questions

1. Can I recall a season in my life when I was in "not enough"? What did it feel like?
2. What is in my hands right now that I need to place in God's hands for multiplication?
3. Do my words and thoughts reflect survival — or overflow?
4. How does Jason's testimony of moving from food stamps to sowing my faith for my future?
5. What does "my cup runs over" (Psalm 23:5 NKJV) mean to me personally?
6. Which stage best describes my current life — Egypt, the wilderness, or the Promised Land?

⚐ Closing Prayer

Father, I thank You for being the God of more than enough. Forgive me for the times I settled for not enough or just enough. Today, I place what I have in Your hands and trust You to multiply it. I declare that I am moving out of lack and into overflow.

My cup runs over, not just for myself, so I can bless others and advance Your Kingdom.

In Jesus' name, Amen.

Next Chapter Teaser

When you understand that God is able to take you from not enough to more than enough, your faith begins to stretch beyond limitations. But here's the ultimate key: none works without God Himself. In the next chapter, we'll uncover why if God doesn't work, nothing works — and how trusting His Word alone positions you for supernatural increase.

CHAPTER 8

IF GOD DOESN'T WORK, NOTHING WORKS!

Hook

Have you ever come to a place in life where you knew — without a doubt — that if God didn't show up, you were finished? That was me. I had exhausted every option, and there was no plan B. Either God was going to move on His Word, or I was going to sink.

That's when I learned one of the most powerful truths of my life: If God doesn't work, nothing works.

My Story

When I started sowing, I had nothing left to lean on but God. My attitude was simple: "Lord, if this doesn't work, I'm finished." I wasn't playing games. I knew that only God could turn my poverty around. And if He was the one telling me to give, then I was going all in.

I didn't have people lining up to bless me back then. I didn't have wealth, investments, or financial security. But I had God's Word — and that was enough.

Today, I look back with amazement. The principle I once tested in desperation has now become the foundation of my prosperity. People sow into my ministry every single day, day and night. Why? Because God's Word never fails.

And here's what still blows my mind: in the past 8 years, Ramona and I, in addition to our daily seed, have sown three one-time seeds that I could never have imagined sowing when I first started. Twice, we sowed $50,000 into a mighty and prosperous man of God, and once into our church. Then in July 2022, after my heart transplant, the Lord gave me a vision and instructed me to sow a one-time seed of $55,555.00 into my spiritual father.

At first, I was stunned by the exactness of that number. But then God began to open my eyes. Biblically, the number 5 represents grace. Five stacked fives spoke prophetically of supernatural grace multiplied — grace upon grace upon grace. It was as if God was declaring that the same grace that spared my life through a heart transplant was now being multiplied into every area of my future: my family, my ministry, my finances, and my destiny.

When I started sowing in 2007, I could have never imagined that I would sow a seed of over $50,000 someday. But God cannot lie. His Word is accurate. And I stand here as a living witness — He will do the same for you, or greater, based upon the seeds you sow in faith.

Scripture & Teaching

1. God's Word Cannot Fail – "For with God nothing will be impossible" (Luke 1:37 NKJV). If God says it, it must come to pass. His Word is not a suggestion — it's a guarantee.
2. God Cannot Lie – "God is not a man, that He should

lie, nor a son of man, that He should repent. Has He said, and will He not do? Or has He spoken, and will He not make it good?" (Numbers 23:19 NKJV). Man's promises may fail, but God's promises are eternal.

3. The Law of the Harvest – "Remember that the person who plants few seeds will have a small crop; the one who plants many seeds will have a large crop" (2 Corinthians 9:6 GNT). God tied increase to sowing. If you want a harvest, you must release seed. The measure you give determines the measure you receive.

Practical Faith Actions

1. Identify Your "All In" Seed – Ask God what seed He wants you to sow in this season. It may not be large compared to others, but it must be significant to you. Remember, it's not the size of the seed — it's the faith and obedience behind it that moves God.

2. Name Your Seed and Remember This Principle – Don't just give randomly — sow with purpose. Write down the scripture you're standing on (Luke 1:37 NKJV, Numbers 23:19 NKJV, or 2 Corinthians 9:6 GNT) and attach it to your seed. Then remind yourself of this Kingdom law: what you sow into, you grow into. When you sow into abundance, you grow into abundance. When you sow into ministry, you grow into the anointing on that ministry and the minister. And never forget this truth: when you sow into a prophet, you will prosper (2 Chronicles 20:20 NKJV). Your seed is not leaving your life — it's entering your future.

3. **Expect Grace Multiplied** – As I saw with the prophetic number 5, your seed carries meaning. Begin to confess daily, "God's grace is multiplied in my life. His favor surrounds me like a shield. My seed guarantees my harvest." Live with expectation, because faith is the bridge that carries your seed into manifestation.

✔ Summary

- Without God, nothing works. With God, everything changes.
- My journey of sowing started with desperation but has grown into sowing tens of thousands of dollars in faith today.
- In 2021, I sowed $55,555 — a seed prophetically marked by the number 5, representing God's grace multiplied for supernatural breakthrough.
- Luke 1:37 (NKJV) guarantees that God's Word never returns void.
- Numbers 23:19 (NKJV) assures us that God cannot lie — if He said it, He will perform it.
- 2 Corinthians 9:6 (GNT) reveals the law of increase: you reap according to the measure you sow.
- What God did for me; He will do for you — or greater — based on your faith and your seed.

✒ Reflection Questions

1. Have I ever reached a point in life where I realized only God could turn things around?
2. What is one area of my life where I need to trust God's Word fully?
3. How does Jason's testimony of extensive seed sowing stretch my faith for my financial future?
4. Am I sowing sparingly or generously? What harvest am I preparing for?
5. How does the truth that "what you sow into, you grow into" shift my perspective on giving?

⚖ Closing Prayer

Father, I acknowledge today that without You, nothing works. Forgive me for the times I've tried to rely on my own strength or the systems of this world. I put my complete trust in Your Word, because it cannot fail. You are not a man that you should lie — every promise you've spoken will come to pass.

Lord, help me to sow faithfully and generously, knowing that You are the God of the harvest. I declare that my future is secure, not in my ability, but in Your unshakable Word.

In Jesus' name, Amen.

Next Chapter Teaser

When you realize that God's Word cannot fail, you are more confident in taking bold steps of faith. In the next chapter, we'll uncover how obedience to God's voice opens doors no man can shut and brings you blessings that your effort could never achieve.

CHAPTER 9

THE PROOF OF MINISTRY

Hook

How do you measure the success of a ministry? Is it in the size of the building, the number of followers, or the minister's lifestyle? No. The valid proof of a ministry is not what the minister has — it's what the people who follow them have.

My Story

When God began teaching me the laws of sowing and reaping, I quickly realized this principle wasn't just for me — it was for those I was called to lead. One day in prayer, the Lord spoke to me clearly:

"The proof of a person's ministry is not what they have — it's what the people have that follow them."

That word pierced my spirit. I could not stand before people and preach prosperity if it only worked for me but never showed up in their lives.

In fact, I remember praying with tears: "Father, don't let these people sow into me unless You are going to bless them. I don't want to receive a seed unless it produces a harvest in their lives."

And that's precisely what God did. As members started

sowing into me, their lives went from nowhere to somewhere. Seismic things began to happen in their lives. Breakthroughs started coming from unexpected places. Many of my members now travel with me and boldly testify of how dramatically their lives and incomes have changed since they began sowing a daily seed.

That became the proof for me — that the Word was working. It wasn't just blessing me; it was lifting them. That's true Kingdom ministry.

Scripture & Teaching

1. Fruit in the Followers – Jesus said, "By this My Father is glorified, that you bear much fruit; so you will be My disciples" (John 15:8 NKJV). The glory isn't in how much the leader shines — it's in how much fruit the people bear.

2. Paul's Example – Paul didn't boast about his wealth; he boasted about his churches' spiritual and financial growth. He wrote, "Not that I seek the gift, but I seek the fruit that abounds to your account" (Philippians 4:17 NKJV).

3. The Elijah Principle – When the widow sowed into Elijah, "she and he and her household ate for many days. The bin of flour was not used up, nor did the jar of oil run dry, according to the word of the Lord" (1 Kings 17:15–16 NKJV). The miracle wasn't just for Elijah — it multiplied in her house. Proof of the prophet's ministry was not in what he had, but in the overflow she received.

Practical Faith Actions

1. Judge Ministry by Fruit, Not Flash – Don't be deceived by outward appearances. Ask: "Are the people being changed? Are lives being lifted?" That's the actual proof of a God-sent ministry.

2. Connect Your Faith to Your Leader's Word – When you sow into a ministry, you're not just supporting an organization — you're drawing from the anointing on that leader. What's on them begins to come on you.

3. Share and Celebrate Testimonies – Your testimony isn't just proof for you — it's proof of the ministry you're connected to. Every victory you share multiplies faith in others.

Summary

- The proof of a ministry is not in the possessions of the minister, but in the prosperity and fruit of the people.

- God told me, "The proof of a person's ministry is not what they have — it's what the people who follow them have."

- I prayed, "Lord, don't let anyone sow into me unless You bless them." And He answered.

- As members began sowing daily, their lives shifted from nowhere to somewhere. Testimonies of dramatic change and increased income confirmed the Word was working.

- John 15:8 (NKJV) reminds us that God is glorified when disciples bear much fruit.

- Philippians 4:17 (NKJV) shows Paul's heart — he sought fruit in the people's accounts, not his own.
- 1 Kings 17:15–16 (NKJV) proves that when you sow into a true prophet, the blessing multiplies in your house.
- Faithful ministry raises people from not enough to more than enough.

Reflection Questions

1. Have I ever judged a ministry by what the leader had instead of the fruit in the people?
2. What fruit can I point to in my own life as evidence of the Word working through my ministry connection?
3. How does my testimony help prove the power of the Word to others?
4. What step can I take to more intentionally connect my faith to the ministry God has placed me under?

Closing Prayer

Father, I thank You that faithful ministry is proven by fruit in the people's lives. Help me never chase appearances but seek Your Kingdom fruit in my life and those around me.

I declare that the anointing I am connected to produces fruit in me — spiritually, financially, and generationally. Let my life be proof of Your Word at work.

In Jesus' name, Amen.

Next Chapter Teaser

You've learned that the proof of ministry is not what the minister has, but what the people receive. In the next chapter, we'll uncover how legacy and generational wealth are part of God's plan — not just for you, but for your and your children's children.

CHAPTER 10

DON'T KEEP SOWING ON THE SAME LEVEL

Hook

Have you ever noticed that some people sow year after year, but nothing seems to change? One main reason is that they keep sowing at the same level.

But if you want to enter a new harvest, you must be willing to enter a new seed level.

My Story

When God began increasing me, He also began challenging me. I heard Him say: "Don't keep sowing on the same level."

That truth changed my whole perspective on giving. For years, I gave what was comfortable. But comfort never produces growth. Seed that doesn't stretch you will never move you — and if it doesn't move you, how can you expect it to move God?

I often tell pastors: "Don't expect your people to do what you are not doing." That's hypocrisy, and God will never endorse it. Leadership means leading by example.

That's why I let my congregation know how much Ramona and I give every Sunday. Periodically, I even tell them the amount of our daily seed—not to brag but to encourage. I remind them, "If God did this for your pastor, who once lived on welfare, what will He do for you?" When they see me stretching my sowing, it gives them faith to stretch theirs. And together, we all move into new harvests.

Scripture & Teaching

1. Seed to the Sower – "Thus says the Lord of hosts: 'Let your hands be strong, you who have been hearing in these days these words by the mouth of the prophets...'" (Zechariah 8:9 NKJV). God gives seed to the sower. If you're willing to sow, He will always put something in your hand.

2. The Seed Shall Be Prosperous – "For the seed shall be prosperous..." (Zechariah 8:12 NKJV). God doesn't give seed for nothing — He gives it with a promise of prosperity. But prosperity only comes when you're willing to plant the seed at a level that stretches your faith.

3. The Widow at Zarephath – In 1 Kings 17:15–16 (NKJV), a widow had only enough meal and oil left for one last meal for her and her son. But she stretched beyond her comfort when Elijah told her to sow it into him first. That one act shifted her life. The jar of meal never ran out, and the oil never failed. When she gave on a new level, she lived on a new level.

4. Solomon's Extravagant Offering – In 1 Kings 3:4–13 (NKJV), Solomon didn't bring a routine offering. He offered 1,000 burnt offerings to the Lord. That night, God visited him in a dream and gave him

wisdom and riches beyond measure. Solomon's seed moved God because it moved him.

5. The Widow's Two Mites—In Mark 12:41–44 (NKJV), Jesus watched people put large sums into the treasury. But He said the widow who gave two mites gave more than them all. Why? because she stretched herself. She gave her all; heaven recognized it as greater than the rest.

Practical Faith Actions

1. Examine Your Seed Level – Ask yourself: "Have I been sowing on the same level year after year?" If your giving no longer challenges you, it's time to increase it.
2. Let the Seed Move You – Don't give what's convenient. Give what requires faith. If it doesn't move you, it won't move God.
3. Lead by Example – Whether you're a pastor, parent, or leader in any sphere, don't expect others to sow bigger while you stay small. Be transparent. Share your testimony and your sacrifices — it will build faith in others.

Summary

- Don't keep sowing on the same level if you want a greater harvest.
- God gives seed to the sower (Zechariah 8:9 NKJV).
- The seed is designed to prosper (Zechariah 8:12 NKJV).

- The widow at Zarephath stretched and saw her provision multiply (1 Kings 17:15–16 NKJV).
- Solomon's extravagant offering unlocked wisdom and wealth (1 Kings 3:4–13 NKJV).
- The widow's two mites moved heaven because it moved her (Mark 12:41–44 NKJV).
- Don't dishonor God with casual giving — He's not a beggar, He's the King.
- Seed that doesn't move you won't move God.
- Leaders must lead by example in sowing so the people can follow with faith.

Reflection Questions

1. Have I been sowing at the same level year after year? What harvest has it produced?
2. Does my current seed move me, or has it become comfortable?
3. If I am a leader, am I modeling the level of sowing I want to see in others?
4. Which of the Bible examples speaks most to me about stretching my seed?
5. How could increasing my level of sowing change my expectations for the next season?

Closing Prayer

Father, I thank You for being the Lord of the harvest. Forgive me for every time I gave casually or stayed on the same level of sowing. Today, I choose to stretch my seed. I will not give you leftovers; I will provide you with my best.

Lord, make my hands strong, and let my seed be prosperous. Help me to lead by example so that others can see what faith in You will produce.

In Jesus' name, Amen.

Next Chapter Teaser

You've just learned you can't keep sowing on the same level if you want a bigger harvest. In the next chapter, we'll discover how God multiplies the seed you sow and why your increase is always tied to your willingness to release.

CHAPTER 11

GOD MULTIPLIES THE SEED YOU SOW

Hook

What if I told you that every seed you've sown has never left your life? It may have left your hand, but it didn't leave your future. No seed is wasted, forgotten, or ignored in God's system. Every seed carries multiplication inside of it, and when you release it by faith, God Himself takes responsibility for the increase.

My Story

When I started sowing, I had no idea how powerful this principle was. At the time, I was just trying to obey God and survive. But as I stayed consistent, I noticed something: my harvests were coming back bigger than the seeds I planted.

One day, the Lord reminded me of 2 Corinthians 9:10 (NKJV):

> "Now may He who supplies seed to the sower, and bread for food, supply and multiply the seed you have sown and increase the fruits of your righteousness."

That's when it hit me: God doesn't just give you seed — He multiplies the seed you sow. My job is obedience. His job is multiplication. And He's really good at His job!

I've watched this truth play out in my own life. I went from sowing a few dollars in the offering plate, to sowing daily seeds, to sowing tens of thousands at a time. And each level of giving brought a multiplied harvest — financial breakthroughs, supernatural debt cancellations, doors of opportunity, and even miraculous favor that money couldn't buy.

Scripture & Teaching

1. God Supplies and Multiplies – 2 Corinthians 9:10 (NKJV): "Now may He who supplies seed to the sower, and bread for food, supply and multiply the seed you have sown and increase the fruits of your righteousness." Notice — He doesn't just add to your seed, He multiplies it.

2. Isaac's Hundredfold Harvest – Genesis 26:12 (NKJV): "Then Isaac sowed in that land, and reaped in the same year a hundredfold; and the Lord blessed him." Isaac sowed in famine, but God multiplied his seed one hundred times over. The land wasn't favorable, but the God of multiplication was.

3. The Boy's Lunch Multiplied – John 6:11–13 (NKJV): Jesus took five loaves and two fish, gave thanks, and multiplied them until more than 5,000 people ate and were filled — with 12 empty baskets. When you put your little in the Master's hands, it becomes much.

4. The Law of Multiplication – Genesis 1:11 (NKJV): "Then God said, 'Let the earth bring forth grass, the herb that yields seed, and the fruit tree that yields fruit according to its kind, whose seed is in

itself, on the earth'; and it was so." Every seed has reproduction built into it. Apple seeds don't just produce apples — they produce orchards. Corn seeds don't just produce one stalk — they produce a field. In the same way, financial seeds don't just return what you gave — they multiply into more.

Practical Faith Actions

1. Trust God's Math, Not Yours – Stop trying to calculate how God will do it. His multiplication is beyond human logic. Trust that He is working even when you can't see it.
2. Plant Seeds in Famine Seasons – Isaac sowed in famine and reaped a hundredfold. Don't let lack stop you from sowing — your biggest harvests often come from your most sacrificial seeds.
3. Expect Multiplication, Not Addition – Change your mindset. Stop expecting a small return. Begin to declare: "My seed is multiplied, not added to. My harvest is abundant, not minimal."

Summary

- Your seed may leave your hand, but it never leaves your life.
- 2 Corinthians 9:10 (NKJV) promises that God supplies and multiplies the seed you sow.
- Isaac sowed in famine and reaped a hundredfold (Genesis 26:12 NKJV).
- Jesus multiplied the boy's lunch until thousands were fed (John 6:11–13 NKJV).

- Every seed carries reproduction within it (Genesis 1:11 NKJV).
- God doesn't do addition — He does multiplication.

✍ Reflection Questions

1. Can I think of a time when a small seed I sowed came back to me multiplied?
2. Do I tend to expect addition or multiplication from God?
3. What "famine" season am I facing right now where I can sow in faith like Isaac?
4. How does the truth that God multiplies my seed change the way I look at giving?

🙏 Closing Prayer

Father, thank You that You are the God of multiplication. Forgive me for the times I limited You by expecting little. Today, I release my seed into Your hands, trusting You to multiply it.

Just as You multiplied Isaac's seed in famine and the boy's lunch in Galilee, I believe You are multiplying my seed right now. I receive overflow harvests that glorify You and bless generations.

In Jesus' name, Amen.

CHAPTER 12

A DAILY SEED BRINGS A DAILY HARVEST

Hook

You've walked with me through my journey — from food stamps to financial overflow, from welfare to wealth, from a dying heart to a brand-new one. But the real story isn't just about me. It's about the principle that changed my life and will change yours: a daily seed brings a daily harvest.

God's Word cannot fail. The law of seedtime and harvest will never stop working. And if you dare to practice it every day, your life will never be the same again.

My Story Tied Together

Looking back, I see the thread that carried me through every season:

- When I had nothing, I started with a seed.
- When I needed breakthrough, I planted a seed.
- My seed was already in the ground when I was desperate for a new heart.

And every single time, God came through.

From the moment I began sowing daily, my life shifted

from cycles of struggle into cycles of increase. And I know — without a doubt — if He did it for me, He will do it for you.

Scripture & Teaching

1. The Law That Never Fails – "While the earth remains, seedtime and harvest... shall not cease" (Genesis 8:22 NKJV). Seasons change. Economies rise and fall. But this law never fails.
2. The Seed Determines the Harvest – "Do not be deceived, God is not mocked; for whatever a man sows, that he will also reap" (Galatians 6:7 NKJV). Your tomorrow is hidden in the seed you sow today.
3. Your Seed Guarantees Your Future – "He who continually goes forth weeping, bearing seed for sowing, shall doubtless come again with rejoicing, bringing his sheaves with him" (Psalm 126:6 NKJV). Every seed carries a guarantee of joy if you keep sowing.

Challenge

Don't just read this book and put it back on the shelf. Live it.

- Set aside a daily financial seed — no matter how small.
- Sow into fertile, proven Kingdom soil.
- Stretch beyond comfort into faith.
- Declare every day: "Wealth and riches are in my house. My cup runs over. I am blessed to be a blessing."

Your seed will tell your story. And your harvest will become the testimony that others need to see.

Final Summary

- A seed is never lost — it's multiplied into your future.
- Daily sowing creates daily harvests.
- The measure you give determines the measure you live on.
- Your seed will break cycles of lack and establish cycles of abundance.
- God is no respecter of persons — what He did for me, He will do for you.

Reflection Questions

1. What amount will I commit to sow today?
2. Am I ready to stretch beyond comfort into a new level of sowing?
3. Who in my life will be impacted by the harvest my seed produces?

Closing Prayer

Father, I thank You for revealing the power of the seed. Today, I commit to living by this unbreakable principle. I will sow daily, faithfully, and joyfully. I believe that every seed I release multiplies into my future.

I declare that my days of not enough are over. From this

day forward, I step into more than enough — overflow, abundance, and generational blessing. My seed guarantees my harvest, and my harvest will glorify You.

In Jesus' name, Amen.

Final Word to the Reader

This is your moment. Don't wait for perfect conditions — start sowing today. And as you do, get ready to step into the greatest season of your life.

Because a daily seed will bring a daily harvest.

CHAPTER 13

THE TITHE IS FOR PROTECTION, THE OFFERING IS FOR PROVISION

(The Tithe You Owe, The Offering You Choose)

Hook

Have you ever wondered why some believers stay protected, while others seem to live in increase and overflow? The difference often comes down to tithes and offerings.

The tithe is not generosity—it's obedience. It belongs to the Lord. When you return it, you step under His covenant of protection. The offering is also required, but unlike the tithe, there is no fixed amount. God leaves it to you to decide the measure of your giving. And your offering is what unlocks provision.

This is one of the greatest financial keys in the Kingdom: the tithe you owe is the offering you choose.

My Story

For years, I thought that if I tithed, I had done all God required. But the Lord corrected me: "Son, the tithe isn't giving—it's returning. You can't give Me what's already

Mine. And your offering isn't optional—it's the seed you choose to sow."

That shifted everything. The tithe secured my protection, but my offering determined the level of my harvest.

I'll never forget when God told me, "Start matching your offering with your tithe." At that time, my offerings were inconsistent and small. But when I stepped out in faith and gave beyond the tithe, my financial life changed. God began to multiply my seed, increase my resources, and pour out blessings I couldn't contain.

That's when I learned: The tithe is required for protection, the offering is required for provision—but the amount of your offering is up to you.

Scripture & Teaching

1. The Tithe Belongs to the Lord
- "The tithe... is the Lord's; it is holy unto the Lord" (Leviticus 27:30).
- Malachi 3:8–10 shows us that the tithe is non-negotiable—it belongs to Him.
- Returning the tithe is not generosity; it's obedience.

2. The Tithe is for Protection
- "I will rebuke the devourer for your sakes" (Malachi 3:11).
- Tithing keeps the enemy from consuming your finances, draining your resources, or stealing your harvest.

- Think of it like insurance: it doesn't make you wealthy, but it keeps you from loss.

3. The Offering is Required, but the Amount is Optional

- God expects His people to bring offerings, but He doesn't set the percentage.
- "Every man shall give as he is able, according to the blessing of the Lord your God which He has given you" (Deuteronomy 16:17).
- "Let each one give as he purposes in his heart, not grudgingly or of necessity; for God loves a cheerful giver" (2 Corinthians 9:7).
- The offering is required, but God lets you choose the size of your seed.

4. The Offering Unlocks Provision

- "He who sows sparingly will also reap sparingly, and he who sows bountifully will also reap bountifully" (2 Corinthians 9:6).
- "Give, and it will be given to you: good measure, pressed down, shaken together, and running over" (Luke 6:38).
- The measure of your provision is determined by the measure of your offering.

Application: The Master Kingdom Key

When you combine the two, you activate the full financial system of God's Kingdom:

- Tithe = Protection (the devourer is rebuked).

- Offering = Provision (your seed multiplies and brings increase).

If you tithe without giving offerings, you may stay covered, but you won't walk in abundance.

If you give offerings without tithing, you're sowing seed without protection.

But when you do both, you are covered and supplied, sustained and multiplied.

This is a master key in the Kingdom: The tithe you owe, the offering you choose.

Closing Prayer

"Father, thank You for revealing to me this master financial key. I return the tithe in obedience, knowing it secures my protection. I give offerings in faith, knowing they unlock provision. I thank You that while the tithe is fixed, the offering allows me to choose the measure of my seed. I declare that the devourer is rebuked, my resources are covered, and supernatural increase is flowing into my life. In Jesus' name, Amen."

CHAPTER 14

HOW MUCH MONEY IS IN YOUR HEART FOR GOD

Hook:

There comes a defining moment in every believer's life when God asks a question that shakes the core of your heart—not your wallet.

That question is this:

"How much money is in your heart for Me?"

Not how much is in your account. Not how much is in your wallet. But how much is in your heart.

Because until money lives in your heart for God, it will never remain in your hand for man.

I would have never imagined that one day I would be able to honor the Lord and His servant with a gift of fifty thousand dollars or more. That seemed like a dream far beyond my reach. But by the grace of God—and by working these same seedtime and harvest principles that I'm teaching you—I have been able to do this not once, but three times. And I'm already positioned to give much, much more in the near future.

This isn't bragging—it's evidence that the Word works when you work it.

When money is in your heart for God, He will fill your hands in ways you've never dreamed or imagined.

Because money doesn't originate in your hands—it originates in your heart.

The Heart of Giving

2 Kings 12:4 (KJV) says:

"And Jehoash said to the priests, All the money of the dedicated things that is brought into the house of the LORD... and all the money that cometh into any man's heart to bring into the house of the LORD."

Notice that it didn't say, "All the money that cometh into any man's hand," but "into any man's heart."

Before money ever shows up in your hand, it must first take residence in your heart.

God plants giving desires before He releases financial supply.

That's why when your heart becomes generous toward God, He will find ways to flow resources through you.

He will never give you amounts of money that are not already in your heart to give to Him.

He doesn't trust unprepared hearts with unlimited harvests.

He gives seed to the sower, not the storer.

When your heart is full of His purpose, your hands will be full of His provision.

God Knows the Heart

God knows your heart better than you do. He looks past your words and examines your motives.

<u>Luke 12:34 (KJV) says,</u>

"For where your treasure is, there will your heart be also."

And Matthew 6:21 (KJV) repeats the same truth word for word.

It's as if Jesus was saying, "Pay attention! This principle governs everything in the Kingdom."

In the world, money follows manipulation.

But in the Kingdom, money follows hearts, not mouths.

You can talk big faith, but God responds to heart faith.

You can say, "Lord, if I had more, I'd give more," but if you're not faithful to give where you are now, you'll never be faithful when you have more.

If stinginess rules your heart, increase will only magnify your greed.

If generosity rules your heart, increase will multiply your giving.

That's why God starts with the heart before He ever talks about harvest.

When Money Isn't in Your Heart for God

Here's a raw truth—and raw truth is never popular:

When money is not in your heart for God, it will not be in your hand for man.

That means if generosity toward God isn't part of your heart posture, then provision for others will never flow through your hands.

Why? Because the flow of divine provision is blocked at the heart level, not the bank level.

Many in the Body of Christ are not Kingdom-minded.

They are denomination-minded, church-minded, or tradition-minded—but not Kingdom-minded.

They shout and dance but still live broke, not because God hasn't blessed them, but because they've never learned to sow from the heart.

Religion teaches you to hold on.

The Kingdom teaches you to let go—so that increase can flow.

When God finds a giver, He finds a channel.

When He finds a channel, He finds someone He can trust with overflow.

The Principle of Increase

<u>2 Corinthians 9:10 (NLT) declares:</u>

"For God is the one who provides seed for the farmer and then bread to eat. In the same way, He will provide and increase your resources and then produce a great harvest of generosity in you."

It starts with God providing seed. But He doesn't give that seed to just anyone—He gives it to the farmer, the one who intends to sow.

If you want God to entrust you with more, you must first prove faithful with what He's already placed in your hand.

Every dollar is a test of your trust. Every paycheck is an opportunity to show your heart posture.

When you honor God with your tithe and your seed, you declare:

"Lord, I trust You more than I trust my paycheck."

And when God sees that, He multiplies the seed sown—not just back to you, but through you.

Seek God and Live

<u>Amos 5:6 (MSG) says:</u>

"So seek GOD and live! You don't want to end up with nothing to show for your life but a pile of ashes..."

That's a sobering word.

So many people will work their entire lives and have nothing to show for it because they never sought God with their heart—or their finances.

They chased wealth but missed purpose. They gained possessions but lost seed.

When you seek God, you live—financially, spiritually, and eternally.

When you make Him your source, your harvest will never die.

Everything connected to you starts thriving when your giving honors God.

When God Has to Beg You to Give

Here's a truth that will shake you:

> If God has to beg you to give through your pastor, you will always be broke.

God will never bless a disobedient heart.

Giving is not God's way of taking from you—it's His divine method of getting more to you.

When you resist giving, you're not protecting your money—you're blocking your miracle.

When giving becomes a debate instead of a delight, you close the very door that releases abundance.

The moment you start arguing with God about what to give, you've already delayed your harvest.

Obedience is the key that unlocks overflow.

A Kingdom Heart Brings a Kingdom Harvest

Your future harvest is hidden in the condition of your heart right now.

If you'll get money in your heart for God—He will put money in your hand for man.

He will use you as a vessel to fund His Kingdom, build His house, and bless His people.

Your job is to keep your heart pure, your motives right, and your giving consistent.

Don't let greed, fear, or fatigue contaminate your seed.

God doesn't just want to bless you; He wants to bless through you.

When He finds a heart that loves Him, He will find hands that lack nothing.

Prayer

Heavenly Father,

Search my heart today. Remove anything that would block the flow of generosity.

Teach me to give with joy, to sow with faith, and to trust You fully.

Fill my heart with Your purpose so my hands can carry Your provision.

Let every seed I sow produce a harvest that glorifies You and expands Your Kingdom.

In Jesus' mighty name, Amen.

CONCLUSION

Best-Seller Conclusion:

From Seed to Signature Harvest — Now It's Your Turn
You've learned the laws. You've heard my story. You've written your reflections and taken faith actions. Now sign your harvest with your habits. Faith without works is dead, but faith with daily sowing becomes compounding obedience.

Start today—again. If you missed yesterday, sow today. If you reaped a great harvest, sow again on a higher level. Remember: the tithe is God's unchanging claim on the firstfruits (protection), and your offerings are your vote for a bigger future (provision). Sow where you want to go. Partner with God, steward the harvest, bless others, and keep your hands strong (Zechariah 8:9–12).

I am praying over your 30-, 60-, and 100-fold testimonies. The same God who moved me from welfare to millionaire will reveal your next instruction, your next seed, and your next field. Obey quickly. Sow joyfully. Reap gratefully. Then repeat.

THE 30-DAY SEED CHALLENGE

Why a Challenge?

Reading this book is only the beginning. The real transformation happens when you put these principles into practice. A 30-day challenge creates momentum, consistency, and faith expectancy. Remember, a seed doesn't just leave your hand—it enters your future.

The 30-Day Commitment

For the next 30 days, commit to sowing something every single day. The amount isn't the focus—the obedience and faith are. Some days it may be $1, some days $10, other days $100 or more. The key is: every day, put a seed in the ground.

Step 1: Decide Your Daily Seed
- Pray and ask God what your daily seed should be.
- It must move you. If it doesn't move you, it won't move God.
- Write down your daily seed goal (example: $10 a day for 30 days).

Step 2: Name Your Seed
- Attach a purpose to your seed. Write down the harvest you're believing for: financial breakthrough, debt cancellation, healing, business growth, family restoration, etc.
- Back it up with a scripture (example: Philippians 4:19, Luke 6:38, or 2 Corinthians 9:6-10).

Step 3: Sow with Intention
- Don't give casually. Every day, sow prayerfully and faithfully.
- Speak over your seed: "God, I thank You this seed is multiplying in my life. My daily seed is bringing me a daily harvest."

Step 4: Keep a Seed Journal
- Record the date, the amount you sowed, the scripture you attached, and what you're believing for.
- Document every testimony, no matter how small. Small harvests are proof that bigger ones are on the way.

Step 5: Expect Multiplication
- Don't just expect addition—expect multiplication.
- Live in daily expectation. Wake up saying, "My harvest is coming today!"
- Celebrate every breakthrough along the way.

Reflection Questions for the Challenge

1. What seed am I committing to sow daily for the next 30 days?
2. What scripture am I attaching to my seed?
3. What harvest am I believing for at the end of this challenge?
4. How will I testify when God multiplies my seed?

Closing Word

This 30-Day Seed Challenge isn't about money but about faith, consistency, and obedience. By the end of 30 days, you won't just have sown 30 seeds—you'll have planted 30 futures. And as you stay faithful, your testimony will shout the truth of this book:

☞ A daily seed will bring a daily harvest.

ABOUT THE AUTHOR

Dr. Jason Martin Sr.

Dr. Jason Martin Sr. is a dynamic Christian leader, recording artist, pastor, and financial empowerment mentor whose life embodies transformation through faith and Kingdom principles. With over 30 years of ministry experience, he has dedicated his life to teaching the power of seedtime and harvest—principles that took him from welfare to multimillionaire status.

A prolific recording artist with 11 gospel albums, Dr. Martin's music reflects his passion for worship and his commitment to spreading the message of hope, healing, and breakthrough. He also hosted a gospel radio broadcast for four years and served as a television host on Seattle's TBN affiliate, expanding his influence across airwaves and platforms.

Dr. Martin's testimony is one of divine intervention and resilience. In March 2021, after being told it could take up to five years to receive a heart transplant, he miraculously received a donor heart in just three days. This modern-day miracle has become a cornerstone of his message: God still works wonders for those who believe.

Beyond ministry and music, Dr. Martin's teachings on financial stewardship and giving have empowered countless individuals to break cycles of lack and walk in abundance. His upcoming book, A Daily Seed Will Bring a Daily Harvest, captures the principles that transformed his life and continue to inspire audiences worldwide.

A graduate of the Seattle FBI Citizens Academy and an 8-year U.S. Navy veteran, Dr. Martin brings both discipline and vision to his leadership. He is the founder and senior pastor of Kingdom Church International, where he and his wife Ramona—his partner in life and ministry of 19 years—shepherd their congregation with love, wisdom, and Kingdom focus. Together, they have raised seven children and are building a legacy of faith, family, and generational wealth.

Dr. Martin is living proof that faith, obedience, and consistent sowing can move a person from "not enough" to "more than enough." His life is a demonstration of the power of God to turn adversity into abundance, and his mission is to help others experience the same breakthrough.

www.ingramcontent.com/pod-product-compliance
Lightning Source LLC
Chambersburg PA
CBHW071533120626
46550CB00006B/2446